"In this delightful book, Amy helpfully introduces us to some relativity unfamiliar Bible stories. And when she retells the more familiar ones, her clever and playful use of names and backgrounds makes those stories feel fresh and new, as well!"

**Bob Hartman, storyteller and award-winning author**

For my own Abigail

# Queen Esther, Nation Saver

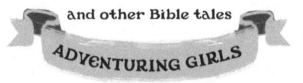

and other Bible tales

ADVENTURING GIRLS

## Amy Scott Robinson

LION
CHILDREN'S

## A note about the Bible stories

Some details of these Bible stories have been retold slightly
differently for the purposes of these adventurous retellings.
Why not look the stories up in their original versions in a
Bible? The notes at the end of each chapter in this book
will tell you where to find them.

Text copyright © 2022 Amy Robinson
This edition copyright © 2022 Lion Hudson IP Limited

Illustrations by Evelt Yanait, Advocate Art Ltd

The right of Amy Robinson to be identified as the author of this work has been
asserted by her in accordance with the Copyright, Designs and Patents Act 1988.

Published by **Lion Children's Books**
www.lionhudson.com

Part of the SPCK Group,
SPCK, 36 Causton Street, London, SW1P 4ST

ISBN 978 0 7459 7953 3
e-ISBN 978 0 7459 7954 0

First edition 2022

**Acknowledgments**
Scripture quotations taken from Revised Standard Version of the Bible, copyright ©
1946, 1952, and 1971 the Division of Christian Education of the National Council of
the Churches of Christ in the United States of America. Used by permission. All rights
reserved.

A catalogue record for this book is available from the British Library

Produced on paper from sustainable sources

Printed and bound in the UK, January 2022, LH26

# *C*ontents

To the reader

Do you know any Bible stories? I wonder which ones they are? There are a few popular ones that seem to get told over and over again, and strangely, they often have men or boys as their main characters. But the Bible is not just one book. It's a library of sixty-six books, all full of amazing adventures and characters – and plenty of them are women and girls.

For this book, I have found some of the stories that aren't told so often. I have no idea why not, because they're great stories. Some are funny, some make you think, and some – like the story of Queen Esther – keep you on the edge of your seat with scares and surprises. And they all star at least one girl.

I've found it really fascinating to learn more about these women and explore their stories, so I've put a little bit at the end of each one to tell you where I found the story, how I retold it, and what it made me think about. I hope you find them interesting too.

Enjoy the adventure!

Amy Scott Robinson

# Miriam's Lullaby

Long ago, in a country far away, there was a king who divided all the people in his country into two groups. There were Bricklayers, who made bricks and built walls; and there were Landowners, who had rich farms and big houses. The Bricklayers had hardly any money, and the Landowners gave them all the most difficult and unpleasant jobs. In fact Bricklayers were so badly treated and so unhappy that the king began to worry that they might try to fight the Landowners. So that they would never have a strong enough army to stand up for themselves, he gave orders to kill all the Bricklayers' newborn baby boys.

In that same country lived a Bricklayer family: a father, a mother called Jochebed, a girl called Miriam, and a baby boy.

At first, Jochebed and Miriam hid the baby inside the house. He fitted neatly inside their big casserole dish with the lid. He sucked quietly on his fingers in the laundry basket under dirty sheets. Once, when a soldier knocked on the door unexpectedly, Miriam managed to hide the baby underneath the cat. But babies grow, and the more he outgrew the hiding places, the more worried Jochebed and Miriam became. They knew they couldn't hide him for ever. Every night as they cuddled him to sleep, they sang to him. It was a song that Miriam made up:

> *Tiny man, we love you so,*
> *Safe and secret may you grow,*
> *Where you are, let no one know!*
> *Sleep peacefully! Sleep peacefully!*

The terrible day came when Jochebed heard the soldiers coming through the village again, and knew that they had nowhere to hide the baby. She had to think quickly. Taking a big basket, she smeared the outside with tar to make it waterproof. Then she placed the baby inside the basket and closed the lid. She called Miriam.

"Take your baby brother down to the river," she

said, trying to hold back her tears. "Put the basket in the water and let him float downstream. We will have to hope that he travels to a place where he will find kindness, for we can't look after him here safely any longer."

She thrust the basket into Miriam's arms and turned away, no longer able to hold back her sobs.

Miriam took the basket and left the house. She hadn't gone far when she met the soldiers.

"What have you got in that basket, little Bricklayer girl?" their leader asked roughly.

"Nothing! I mean, nothing yet," said Miriam, thinking on her feet. "I'm going to the river to gather reeds for weaving."

"Working hard, just as a Bricklayer should," said the soldier approvingly, and let her past.

When Miriam reached the river, she climbed down the bank and carefully placed the basket on the water. The baby stirred, so Miriam sang to him, and as she sang new words floated into her head:

> *Tiny man, I love you so,*
> *Safe and secret may you grow*
> *Floating on the river's flow!*
> *Sleep peacefully! Sleep peacefully!*

Just then, she looked across to the opposite bank, and a big clump of reeds caught her eye. Her first thought was that she should gather some, in case the soldiers checked when she returned. Then she noticed how the rushes grew out into the water, and she had another thought. What if she wedged the basket there? It might stay hidden and not float away, and perhaps she would be able to come back and collect her brother later. Sliding quickly down the bank, she waded into the river, rescued the basket again, and pulled it into the reeds.

Miriam couldn't quite bring herself to leave the baby all alone. What if the basket tipped or began to sink? She crouched down so that the reeds covered her head. Nobody would see her if she waited here for a while. She stared at the little basket and began to wonder what she would do if a crocodile came along – she had seen them in the river before. To keep herself and her brother calm, she began to sing again:

> *Tiny man, we love you so,*
> *Safe and secret may you grow,*
> *Stay unharmed by every foe,*
> *Sleep peacefully! Sleep peacefully!*

The song, the sunshine, the rippling water, and the rustling reeds were all very soporific, and Miriam felt her eyes closing, but she was startled awake by a splashing sound. She peeped out of the reeds, expecting to see a crocodile or maybe even a hippopotamus. To her surprise, what she saw was a woman's legs, standing quite close to the hidden basket. The woman they belonged to was washing in the river. Miriam looked up – and clapped a hand over her mouth to stop herself from screaming.

It was the princess! The king's own daughter! This was a disaster! If she found the baby, she would surely take him straight to the king and have him killed! Miriam desperately tried to work out what to do, but it was too late. The splashing was rocking the basket, and the baby woke up and started to cry.

"What's this?" The princess parted the reeds and looked down at the basket. Miriam bit her lip. The princess reached down, opened the lid, and gasped.

"Hello, little one! Who's left you here?" The royal face had softened into a look of concern. "Are you one of those Bricklayer baby boys that my father has been murdering? Yes, that must be it. And some poor Bricklayer woman has abandoned you here. What a shame! Poor little baby!"

The princess scooped Miriam's baby brother up out of the basket and held him in her arms. "I wish I could take you home with me. I haven't got a little baby of my own." She gazed into the baby's face, and he stopped crying.

A plan flew into Miriam's head like a kingfisher diving into a stream. She stood up, poking her head out above the reeds and startling the princess.

"Your Majesty, why don't you take this baby? He clearly needs someone to look after him. You could bring him up as a Landowner, as if he were your own son."

"You know, little girl, I think I will do that!" exclaimed the princess.

"There's only one little problem, of course," Miriam continued. "He looks too little to have proper food yet. He will still need a mother's milk to grow big and strong."

The princess was crestfallen. "Oh, you're right," she said. "I don't have any babies, so I can't feed him myself."

"Hmmm, that's a pity. Oh, I have an idea!" said Miriam, pretending it had only just occurred to her. "What if I go and find a Bricklayer woman who has just had a baby? She would be able to feed him for you until he's big enough."

"That's a good idea! Go ahead, little Bricklayer girl. When you find such a woman, bring her to me at the palace," said the princess.

Miriam didn't need telling twice. She raced away from the river, into the village, and back to her mother. Jochebed was cleaning the house, the tears still making rivers down her cheeks. When she saw Miriam's delighted face, she stopped what she was doing and listened as the flood of words poured out.

At the end of her story, Miriam finished breathlessly, "So who shall I bring to nurse the little prince while he grows up safely? YOU, of course!"

Jochebed swept her clever daughter up in her arms and danced around the room with her.

So Miriam and Jochebed stayed with their little baby boy while he grew. Jochebed fed him and snuggled him, Miriam rocked him and bounced him. And as they did, they sang Miriam's song to him:

> *Tiny man, we love you so,*
> *Safely as a prince you'll grow,*
> *Peace and freedom may you know!*
> *Live happily! Live happily!*

---

**Where does this story come from?**

*This story can be found right at the beginning of the book of Exodus. It's not the only story about Miriam: she grew up to be a poet and musician and, much later on, she helped her grown-up little brother, Moses, to lead all their people across a sea with a song.*

---

## What does it make you think about?

*Miriam's caring and quick thinking saved her brother's life, which is a wonderful thing in itself: but because of her actions, Moses was able to grow up and free all God's people from slavery in Egypt. This shows me that when it comes to being part of God's story, there are no more important and less important people. Everyone is important, and Christians believe that everyone fits in to God's plan. The kind action you do today may still be making an enormous difference even years later.*

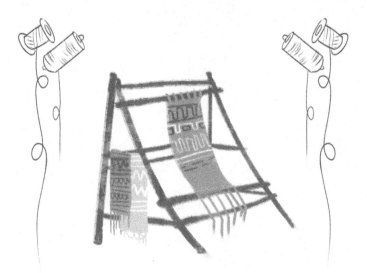

# The Five Sisters

Tirzah sat at the loom weaving cloth, back and forth, back and forth. It took a lot of cloth to dress five sisters and keep their tent warm and waterproof, and weaving it was Tirzah's happiest job. All day she sat, sending the shuttle back and forth, back and forth; dreaming and weaving and watching the cloth grow longer.

When her two older sisters, Milcah and Mahlah, came to talk to Tirzah, they talked about men and marriage and business. They told her what was going on outside, what new instructions had been given, whether they would soon be packing up and journeying through the wilderness again; and all the while the shuttle went back and forth, back and forth, and the cloth grew longer.

When her two little sisters, Noa and Hoglah, came to play with Tirzah, they danced around her and sang songs. Tirzah told them stories about their people, about their journey, about their God; and all the while her shuttle went back and forth, back and forth, and the cloth grew longer.

One day, Milcah and Mahlah came in looking excited and worried.

"The men are in the Tent of Meeting," said Milcah, "and I think that we will soon be arriving in the Promised Land. This place we've dreamed about and journeyed toward all our lives – I can hardly believe that we will get to see it!"

"How do you know we're so close?" asked Tirzah, as her shuttle flew across the cloth.

"Because they are deciding how the land will be divided up between all the sons of the families who escaped from Egypt," Mahlah explained, "so that for every family that started the journey, there will be a place to stay and call their own."

"All the sons?" asked Tirzah, stopping her weaving to look into her big sister's face.

"Only the sons," said Mahlah.

"But that's not fair. Our father and mother died on the journey, and we have no brothers. Where are we supposed to live?"

The two big sisters shrugged and shook their heads. Tirzah set her shuttle flying again, back and forth, back and forth. The cloth grew some more. Into the tent rolled the two little sisters, in a dancing cloud of sand and laughter.

"Tell us a story, Tirzah!" begged Noa and Hoglah, who never sat still unless they were listening to one of Tirzah's tales.

Tirzah thought as she wove in another colourful thread. "Have I ever told you the story of how our leader, Moses, helped our people to escape from Egypt?"

"Yes, lots of times," said Noa. "The one with the frogs and the locusts."

"No, it's the one with the sea that stood up and let everyone walk through!" said Hoglah.

"Before all of that," said Tirzah, "the mean king of Egypt had made our people slaves. They had to work all day making bricks. Moses knew it was unfair to treat people that way. He knew that God wanted him to speak up. But he didn't want to do it! He was too scared."

The two big sisters sat down with the little ones.

"What did he do?" asked Noa.

"He asked his brother to come with him, because everything feels safer when you have your family with you. And the two of them went to the mean king, and even though Moses was shaking like a tent in the wind, he said: 'Let my people go!'"

"And THEN it's the bit with the frogs," said Noa.

"So it is, clever girl," said Tirzah, and she stood up from her loom, leaving the shuttle dangling from its coloured thread. "Listen: Moses knew something was unfair, and he took his brother and spoke up about it, even though he was scared. Now we know that something is unfair, we should take our sisters and speak up about it. Moses won't turn us away."

Two big sisters and two little sisters stared at Tirzah with wide eyes.

"You mean... go to the Tent of Meeting?" asked Milcah.

"Us?" gasped Mahlah.

"To see real, live Moses?" said Noa.

"To ask him for something?" wondered Hoglah.

But Tirzah was already halfway out of the tent, and her "Yes!" was shouted to the open air. The sisters looked at one another in surprise and followed her: out of their tent, through the camp, past all the other women who were cooking and nursing their babies, and straight to the Tent of Meeting where the men sat.

As they walked through the outer courtyard of the Tent of Meeting, the place fell silent and everybody turned to look. Five sisters made their way across the courtyard to the Tent's entrance where Moses' brother and the priests and all the important ones were, making decisions; and there was Moses himself, with his grey hair and beard and his wise, tired eyes. In his hand was the long walking stick from all Tirzah's stories: the stick that had turned into a snake, parted the sea, and knocked water out of a rock, all because God said so. The little sisters stared at it.

Tirzah gave a nervous cough, which sounded very loud to her, and began: "Sir, we know that you're dividing up the land between the sons of those who journeyed from Egypt, but only the sons."

Mahlah reached out for Tirzah's hand and squeezed it for courage.

"Sir, our father died on the journey. He had five daughters, no sons." She faltered, unsure how to carry on. Moses waited. Milcah took Mahlah's other hand and spoke up.

"It's not fair for our father's daughters not to receive a place in the land he set out for. Please give us part of this Promised Land too."

"Not fair!" agreed Noa, taking Milcah's hand and holding her other one out to Hoglah.

"And frogs!" pronounced Hoglah, who wanted to join in.

Moses looked at the sisters standing hand in hand in front of him. He closed his eyes and talked to God for what seemed like a very long time, and when he opened them again, he was smiling.

"God says that you are right," Moses told them. "And there will be land, not just for you, but for any other women in the same situation; and not just for now, but always. Because of your courage and wisdom, this will become one of our laws from now on."

Sometime later, in a house built firm in the Promised Land, Tirzah sat at her loom. When her older sisters came to see her, Milcah talked about her wedding plans and Mahlah brought her new baby. And when her younger sisters came to see her, Tirzah had a new tale to tell; and as they told it together, she sent her shuttle back and forth, back and forth, and the cloth grew longer.

---

**Where does this story come from?**

*The five daughters of Zelophehad appear three times in the books of Numbers and Joshua, showing how important their story is at this time in the history of Israel. You can find this story in Numbers 27:1–11. The Bible doesn't tell us very much about each individual sister, not even their ages, but I did find out the meanings of all their names, which helped me to imagine their characters and decide which would be older and younger. Milcah means "queen", Mahlah means "forgiven", and Tirzah means "pleasing", while the two little ones, Noa and Hoglah, mean "movement" and "dancing"!*

---

## What does it make you think about?

*When I read the story in the Bible, I noticed how well the sisters knew their history and law to be able to challenge it in the way that they did. It's not just that they knew they were being treated unfairly; they knew who to talk to about it, and had faith that Moses and God would agree with their case. Knowing about the past can be very valuable in challenging injustice. When you look at the world around you, what do you see happening that is still unfair? Is anybody challenging it? Is there anything that you could do to make the world a fairer place?*

# Mrs Manoah

Mrs Manoah was completely alone when it happened, and for the rest of her life she felt that this was a significant point. She was by herself, in the field with nobody else around, feeding the goats at the same time that she did every morning when she saw the Majestic Man for the first time. Straight away, in her head, she called him the Majestic Man, and from then on that's how she described him: taller and broader than was quite natural, shining with a glow that wasn't explained by the morning sun, and most importantly, knowing exactly where and when to find Mrs Manoah all by herself.

"Greetings, Mrs Manoah," said the Majestic Man. "You're going to have a baby."

"Good heavens!" said Mrs Manoah.

"Precisely," said the Majestic Man. "God wants you to know that your baby son will be rather special, and he wants me to give you some instructions about how to bring him up so that his life will be dedicated to God. There's a list of things you shouldn't eat and drink while you're pregnant with him. Oh, and this one's important: you mustn't ever cut his hair."

"Got it," said Mrs Manoah. "Just let me write all this down..."

A little later, in the kitchen, Mrs Manoah told Mr Manoah about the Majestic Man and what he had said. Mr Manoah was an anxious little man. He furrowed his brow and chewed his lip.

"Oh dear, oh dear," he said, "that all sounds rather complicated. I think we'd better have a proper sort of meeting with this chap. Get him to sit down and really explain everything we'll have to do."

"It's fine," said Mrs Manoah. "He was perfectly clear. I've got it all written down right here."

"Well, I really think I should hear it too, just in case," said Mr Manoah, "or, oh dear, we'll be in a terrible muddle."

"There's no muddle," said Mrs Manoah. "I have the instructions right here."

But Mr Manoah was already leaving the room on his way to say a prayer demanding an urgent meeting with God's messenger.

A couple of days later, the Majestic Man appeared in the field again, choosing (as Mrs Manoah would later like to point out) exactly the same time of day, when she was all alone feeding the goats.

"Is there a problem?" he said kindly. "I was asked to come again. Did I not explain properly the first time?"

"It's not me," sighed Mrs Manoah, "It's my husband. He wants to hear it with his own ears."

"Oh. How unusual. Well, if you don't mind, you'd better go and get him," said the Majestic Man.

Mr Manoah came out carrying a clipboard and wearing a pencil behind his ear, looking very businesslike.

"Now then," he said, "what's all this about my wife having a baby? Tell me everything we need to know. I'll write it all down and make sure it happens."

"I've already told your wife everything she needs to know," said the Majestic Man patiently. "She has a list."

"Right. Well, come in and have lunch with us, and you can tell us all about it," said Mr Manoah.

The Majestic Man exchanged exasperated glances with Mrs Manoah and replied, "I don't eat, actually. If you want to prepare some food, you should send it as a sacrifice to God."

"What's your name, then, so that we know who to thank for all this?" said Mr Manoah briskly, taking the pencil from behind his ear.

"Did you not hear him?" asked Mrs Manoah. "He's already told us who to thank: it's God! Does he look to you like a normal person, with a name, who eats lunch? Honestly! Go and get that sacrifice going."

"She's right," said the Majestic Man. "There's no point in asking my name, because it's wonderful. Too wonderful for you to understand."

"Very well, Mr Wonderful," said Mr Manoah, entirely failing to be awed, "just hang on there while I go and start the fire."

He bustled off. Mrs Manoah and the Majestic Man stood together awkwardly.

"Sorry about him," said Mrs Manoah. "He's a bit... I mean... he likes to be the one in charge."

"So I can see," said the Majestic Man.

Once the fire had got going and the sacrifice was ready, the three of them stood around it, staring into the flames. Mrs Manoah put her hands on her stomach. A baby! After all these years, a little boy of her own! She hadn't needed to write down the instructions. The moment she heard them, they had been engraved in her heart. She would do anything, anything at all, for this little one, this wonderful gift.

She looked over at Mr Manoah, who was poking at the fire. It was likely he would never quite understand what had happened, she realized. Then she looked over at the Majestic Man. Something was happening to him. The fire behind him was making his already shining body glimmer and move and dance like the flame. His feet weren't quite on the floor. Then suddenly he was going up, up like the smoke, and shimmering away into the blue sky.

"Wow," remarked Mr Manoah. "Do you think he might have been an angel?"

"Of course he was, you silly goose," said Mrs Manoah.

"But... but then we're going to die!" Mr Manoah panicked, wringing his hands. "People who see angels of God die!"

Mrs Manoah took hold of her husband's hands. "If God had sent his angel to kill us, dear, I don't think he'd have bothered with all the very specific instructions about how to bring up a baby, do you?"

"Perhaps you're right. Oh, dear!" Mr Manoah looked at his empty clipboard. "I never wrote down what he said."

Mrs Manoah looked skyward for a moment, fancying she could still see, against the sun, the shrinking shape of an exasperated angel.

"Never mind, dear," she replied, "I expect that's why he spoke to me in the first place." And under her breath, as she followed Mr Manoah back into the house, she added, "All alone. By myself. Just me."

---

## Where does this story come from?

*Mrs Manoah is found in the book of Judges, chapter 13. Her son was Samson, a superhumanly strong man with very long hair, and if you read his story you'll see that when a woman called Delilah cut his hair, he lost all his strength; so the Majestic Man's instructions really were very important.*

---

## What does it make you think about?

*I think this is one of the funniest stories in the Bible. I love the way that the angel answers Mr Manoah's prayer by coming a second time to his wife, all alone! Even though the baby was theirs as a couple, Mrs Manoah was the one who was going to have to follow the instructions, and the message was very definitely for her! And even though that makes the story funny, there's a serious point in there too: God speaks to people in individual ways. Nobody can make your decisions about faith and God for you. What your parents or friends believe doesn't have to be the same for you, though they might be able to help by answering your questions; but what you believe about faith is between you and God.*

# Ruth's Big Promise

"Well, girls, this is where we part." The old woman stopped at the crossroads and shifted the heavy bag on her back. "You must go back to your mothers and try to marry again and make a better life. I must go back to my country, and hope that there is still someone living who will look after me."

The two young women she was speaking to hesitated, looking at the old woman and at each other with tears in their eyes. Then one of them turned and walked back the way she had come; but the other one put her arms around the old woman's neck and refused to let go. That special woman's name was Ruth.

Ruth and her mother-in-law, Naomi, had a long way to walk. For the first hour of the journey, Naomi continued trying to persuade Ruth to turn back.

"You will be a foreigner in my country," she said. "There is nothing for you there. I don't yet know whether there will even be anything for me."

But it only made Ruth more determined to keep going.

"Naomi, you've already lost a husband and two sons, and now your other daughter-in-law has walked away from you. I can't let you lose anyone else," she said. "From now on, your country is my country, your family is my family, your God is my God. And if you have nothing, then at least we'll have nothing together."

When at long last they arrived in Naomi's hometown of Bethlehem, it was dark. Naomi sat exhausted on a bench while Ruth knocked on doors and woke up innkeepers to find them a place to stay. It was nearly dawn when the two of them curled up on a single mattress on the floor of a tiny room.

"Get some sleep," whispered Ruth. "Tomorrow I will go and find some food for us. Things will look better soon, you'll see."

It was barely an hour later when Ruth left the sleeping Naomi and crept out of the little room to walk to the fields. Naomi had explained the custom in her country: that when people were poor and without food, they were allowed to walk behind the farmers as they harvested the barley, and pick up any grains that were dropped. Ruth hoped to find a field where she could pick up enough to grind into flour and make a loaf of bread. The first few seemed full of equally hopeful people, but further out from the town there was a quieter field, and Ruth settled herself a good distance behind the harvesters and walked along slowly, scouring the ground for fallen grain.

The sun was high in the sky by the time Ruth had gathered a small handful, and she was just wondering whether she would be able to find something to drink when a shadow fell across her. She looked up to see a tall man sneering down at her, with a little gang of harvesters standing menacingly just behind him.

"We've got a new one," the man said in a low voice. "Another little leech who thinks she can come and grow fat from other people's hard work."

"I... I'm only... I mean, I was told that the custom here..." stammered Ruth.

"The custom here is to be far too nice," snarled the man. "Go back to where you came from."

"Leave her alone!" A second man made his way toward them with big strides. "Not this again, Melech. Stop bothering her."

"You're too soft, Boaz," said the snarling man, turning his attention away from Ruth. "It's not good for business to take in waifs and strays."

"My field, my rules," said Boaz firmly. "God's rules, actually, which you know perfectly well. Now get back to work."

He turned to Ruth as Melech and his cronies grumbled away. "Are you all right? I've noticed you working very hard. Have you found anything?"

Ruth showed him her little handful of grain.

"Poor you – that's not a lot for a morning's work!" said Boaz. "My harvesters are too thorough. Would you like a drink?"

Ruth nodded gratefully.

"Here," said Boaz, offering her a flask from his belt. "And listen, at lunchtime, come and share my bread and dip it in the stew with us. It looks as if you haven't brought anything with you." He smiled kindly.

It was a very happy Ruth who bounced back into the little room that evening, her apron full of barley. As she prepared the meal, she happily told Naomi everything.

"And after lunch, there was so much more grain on the ground – in fact, I think I even saw some of the harvesters pulling bits out of their bundles and dropping them on purpose!" she finished.

"Boaz, did you say his name was? And Melech, the other one? That's interesting, very interesting," mused Naomi.

The harvest went on, and every day Ruth found plenty of barley to take home to Naomi. Melech glowered at her from a distance, but never spoke to her again, and Boaz went on sharing his lunches with Ruth, chatting with her about how she came to be there, and asking after Naomi. Ruth found herself looking forward to seeing Boaz every day, and she felt excited butterflies in her stomach all morning as lunchtime came closer.

One day, the other workers were excited because the harvest was nearly over, and when they brought it in to the threshing floor to be prepared for flour, there was always a big harvest party. They invited Ruth, but she shook her head, suddenly nervous. The custom might allow her to gather grain, but what would Melech say if she turned up to a party? And, even worse, what if Boaz agreed?

"I'm not really one of your workers," she said, "and anyway, I must be at home to take care of Naomi."

Naomi, however, had other ideas when she heard about the invitation.

"Of course you must go to the party," she said. "You've worked so hard, and besides, there's something I need you to do for me there."

"Tell me," said Ruth.

On the evening of the party, Ruth dressed as best she could with the little she had, and sighed at herself in the mirror. Naomi fetched her bag and drew out a tiny bottle.

"This bottle of scented oil was given to me for my wedding day," she said, "and I've kept it safe ever since. It's for you. Put it on, and listen carefully. When you get to the party, don't talk to Boaz until everyone has finished eating and drinking, and he's lying down to sleep. Then I want you to go and wait near him. When he wakes up and notices you, I want you to say – exactly like this – 'Let me wear your cloak, as you are my redeemer.'"

"What does that mean?" asked Ruth.

"You'll see," smiled Naomi. "But don't let anyone hear you or see you talk to him, and come straight back home when he has answered you."

Ruth did as she was told. She enjoyed the harvest party, but kept away from Boaz until everyone was either leaving or lying down to sleep. Boaz, ready to start the threshing early the next day, wrapped himself in his cloak and lay down on the floor. Ruth crept up to him and sat beside him, breathing in the strong smell of Naomi's scented oil and waiting. In the middle of the night, Boaz stirred, turned over, and opened his eyes.

"Ruth! Is that you?"

"Let me wear your cloak," said Ruth, "as you are my redeemer."

"Oh, Ruth!" said Boaz.

"What's the matter? Did I remember it wrong? It's what Naomi told me to say to you," said Ruth.

"Did she? Cunning old Naomi!" smiled Boaz. "She remembers the customs of her country well."

"What does Naomi mean?" asked Ruth.

"Naomi means that, now that her husband and sons are dead, I am the closest relative and can inherit her husband's property – and that means I can marry you, Ruth, if you'll have me."

"Oh, Boaz! Oh, yes!" exclaimed Ruth.

"Unfortunately, Naomi isn't quite right. I am not your closest redeemer. There's a relative older than I am. Your redeemer is Melech."

"Oh, Boaz! Oh, no!" said Ruth.

"Don't worry. I think I know how to deal with him. Go back and tell Naomi that I'm taking care of it," said Boaz.

As she had promised, Ruth slipped out without letting anybody see her, and ran back to Naomi, who had stayed awake waiting and now listened worriedly to Ruth's news.

"We'll go to the town gate tomorrow morning, then," Naomi said.

"Why?" asked Ruth.

"Because that's where these things take place," answered Naomi mysteriously.

The next day, Ruth and Naomi joined a little gathering at the town gate. Boaz and Melech stood in the centre. Boaz spoke first.

"Elders and judges, I am bringing this case because it has come to my attention that Melech is the redeemer for our relative who has died. He leaves an inheritance of a field along with his widow, Naomi. He also leaves the widow of his son, who also died. They are in need of support and help. As the next redeemer in line, I must ask Melech whether he intends to take the inheritance that is his by law."

Melech could hardly believe his luck. "A field! A field of my own! I won't have to work for you any more, Boaz, or follow your stupid rules! Of course I'm taking it!"

"You realize that this inheritance is gained by marrying Ruth?" said Boaz.

Melech scowled. "Fine. Whatever. I'm sure an

extra wife will come in useful around the house."

Ruth's heart sank.

"I don't think you understand," said Boaz. "To be the redeemer means that you carry on the name of the dead man. Ruth's children will inherit. Her family will be your family."

"What? Give up my name and my family for this stranger? Absolutely not!" spat Melech. "Take your precious field and your foreign wife, Boaz."

Then, to Ruth's surprise, he kicked off one of his shoes and held it out to Boaz.

"What's he doing?" whispered Ruth.

"It's a sign that he passes his right to inherit to Boaz," Naomi whispered back gleefully.

Boaz turned to Ruth with a smile. "Come here, my dear."

Ruth stepped forward, and Boaz took her hand as he spoke to the elders.

"In the sight of the elders and judges, I take this woman to be my wife. When she had the chance to stay in her own country, she gave it up to travel with Naomi to a strange place. When she had the chance to go back to her own mother and family, she willingly sacrificed it and promised to be family for Naomi, who was alone. She generously did what you, Melech, failed to do today. She is brave, loving, and worthy, and I promise to love her always."

The crowd cheered and clapped, and Naomi ran forward and swept Ruth into a hug.

"Thank you, Naomi!" Ruth whispered in her ear.

Naomi stepped back, placing both hands on her daughter-in-law's shoulders, and looked into her shining face.

"No, Ruth, thank you. You kept your promise to me. My country is your country, my family is your family, my God is your God. And I thought I had nothing left, but now I know that our God has wonderful things in store for us."

---

## Where does this story come from?

*Ruth has her very own book of the Bible – just look for the book with her name!*

---

## What does it make you think about?

*There is so much kindness in the book of Ruth. It makes me think of how God works in ordinary lives, in families, in sad and happy times, and through simple acts of love. Naomi was absolutely right when she said that God would have more wonderful things in store, because Ruth and Boaz had a son called Obed, who had a son called Jesse, who had a son called David, who became the famous King David in the Bible, the one who killed Goliath; and he, in turn, became an ancestor of Jesus. So through this little family, that began with Ruth leaving her home to be with Naomi, Christians believe that God was building the family of his own Son, who would leave his heavenly home to be with people on earth.*

# Abigail the Unflappable

Prince David was not really a prince.

Like most princes, he knew that he was going to become the next king. He had been chosen for the job when he was still a little boy: anointed by Samuel the Kingmaker, who always knew what he was doing when it came to choosing the next king.

Unlike most princes, though, David was not the son of a king. In fact, he was a shepherd. This was a problem for him, because King Saul, who was still very much alive, was scared that this shepherd prince was going to try to kill him and take his throne straight away. So, Saul decided to strike first by sending out his army after David.

David, who was happy as a shepherd and had no intention of becoming king a moment sooner than necessary, had to find his own army and hide somewhere. He did this very successfully. Nobody in the country knew where he was.

In a farmhouse at the top of a hill, Abigail, the farmer's wife, asked her husband where he thought the prince and all those soldiers had gone.

"They can't have just vanished," she said. "Six hundred men don't just disappear."

"Not interested," grunted Farmer Foole, and raised his newspaper a little higher over his face. "Fetch my slippers."

"Certainly, dear," said Abigail.

The next day, Abigail went to visit the shepherds who were looking after the flocks in the fields at the bottom of the hill. She found rather more of them there than she had expected. In fact, there were nearly as many shepherds as sheep.

"Where have all these people come from?" she asked one of the shepherds that she recognized.

"They're just staying with us for a bit, helping out. They're very good at it. Last night they fought off two wolves and a bear!" the shepherd told her.

That evening, Abigail mused to her husband,

"You know, if I were a shepherd prince in hiding, I think I might hide among other shepherds."

"Makes no sense, woman. A prince would stand out like a sore thumb among shepherds," Farmer Foole retorted, and turned up the radio. "Bring me a cuppa," he added.

"One sugar or two?" asked Abigail.

The next day, Abigail went to collect some sheep and bring them up to the farm to shear their wool. One of the new shepherds was waiting by the field. With a charming smile, he offered to help her separate the wooliest sheep from the flock. She watched him as he skilfully herded the sheep, like the commander of a white, fluffy army. Then, just as he had got them to the gate, somebody across the field shouted to a dog. The shout made the shepherd jump and look over his shoulder, and his sudden movement made the sheep scatter again.

"I'm ever so sorry," said the shepherd. "I'm a little distracted at the moment."

"You do seem a bit jumpy," observed Abigail. "A good shepherd really should be more unflappable."

That evening in the farmhouse, Abigail said, "Prince David must be very scared of being found out. I hope he's chosen a farm where the farmer is good to his workers."

Farmer Foole poked irritably at the fire and rattled the poker loudly on the grate. "Soft-hearted nonsense, woman," he said. "It's no good being nice to people. Makes 'em lazy. Now stop this nonsense about princes and get the dinner on."

"All the same, dear," said Abigail as she fetched a saucepan, "if any shepherd could secretly be a prince, wouldn't that change the way you treated them?"

The day after that, while Farmer Foole went to plough a new field, Abigail stayed at home and began to spin some of the newly shorn wool. She worked until lunchtime, and just as she was sitting down to eat, there was a knock at the door. It was one of the shepherds.

"Mistress Abigail, something terrible has happened!" he gasped. "You know all those new shepherds? They're not who you think they are! They're David and his army in hiding!"

"Well, who'd have thought it?" said Abigail.

"But, Mistress Abigail, the army ran out of food, so Prince David asked Farmer Foole for something to eat; but even though he explained who he really was, Farmer Foole still said no! He said it very rudely, too, and called him names. He said they were a lazy bunch who had probably run away from another farm. And now the prince and his army are on their way up the hillside to kill him, and you, and set the whole farm on fire! Run! We have to hide!"

"Is that so?" said Abigail. "Listen carefully to me, young man, and please do exactly as I say. Go into the kitchen and collect every bit of food we have. Get everything from the larder and the vegetable patch. Load it all up and bring it down to Prince David. I'm going to go and meet him."

With that, Abigail picked up her sandwich, left the house, and set out down the path.

When she heard the thundering of the army on their way up the hillside, Abigail stopped and stood still in the middle of the road. She stood firm on the higher ground as they approached, and apart from a slight lift of her chin, she didn't even twitch as the six hundred soldiers raced toward her. She waited until she was within striking distance of the prince at the front of his army. Then, with serene grace, she bowed. When she lifted her eyes again, not a man moved a muscle. You could have heard a dove folding her wings in the silence.

"Your Majesty," said Abigail, "it's no good sending messages to my husband. He is as foolish as his name. If I had got the message, I would have been here sooner. I have plenty of food for your well-deserving soldiers, and here is some lunch for you." She held out her sandwich.

David held her gaze, but tightened his hand around the grip of his sword.

"Your Majesty, I know that you are going to become king very soon and, more than that, a good king," said Abigail. "When you are king, I'm sure you don't want to be remembered as one who had fits of rage and killed innocent people, all because of a silly man. I'm sure you want to be seen as much more unflappable than that."

"It seems you know plenty about being unflappable," remarked the prince.

"Knowing my husband has taught it to me," replied Abigail with a slight smile, "and I advise you to learn the same in your dealings with him."

Prince David gave a solemn nod, and as he turned to go back down the mountain, he said, "Go in peace."

"Go in peace, O Prince," replied Abigail, taking a bite of the sandwich.

And that was nearly the end of the story, except that when Farmer Foole heard how close he had come to losing everything, and how Abigail had stepped in and stopped an army of hundreds, his heart failed at the shock and he died. When David heard the news, he sent another message to Foolery Farm asking Abigail to be his wife.

This time, the message came straight to Abigail, who was only too happy to change her name from Mrs Foole to Queen Abigail the Wise.

---

## Where does this story come from?

*This story can be found in the book of 1 Samuel, chapter 25. Abigail's husband was called "Nabal", which really does mean "fool". The shepherd prince became King David. There are lots of stories about him, and songs written by him, in the Bible. He was a very good and famous king, though he never learned to be as unflappable in a crisis as Abigail.*

---

## What does it make you think about?

*Because of this story, Abigail is known for both wisdom and courage. Imagine standing your ground in front of an approaching army! Rather than just giving David what he wanted, she made a good argument about why he should not go ahead with his plans of violence. (It's a long speech in the Bible: she talks from verse 24 all the way to verse 31 without stopping!) Her appeal to David changes his mind, brings peace, and prevents bloodshed. We don't need to be big and powerful to stop a fight; gentle and persuasive words do the job even better.*

# Joanna

There was once a poor widow named Joanna who had two children. She loved them very much, but she had no money to look after them. Her husband had been a follower of the holy men, so he had never been at home very much, and when he died he left nothing at all but a lot of debt. He had borrowed money so that he could spend his time up mountains or roaming around, learning from famous holy men like Elisha. Now, the people who had lent him the money wanted it back – and Joanna had nothing to give them.

"I can't manage to feed my children," she told them, "let alone pay back the fortune that my husband spent!"

"We will come back tomorrow," they said, "and if you can't pay by then, we'll take your children as payment instead."

Joanna paced around her tiny house, biting her fingernails, and wondering what to do. Could she run? They had nowhere to go. Could they hide? Not for very long. The more she paced, the angrier she felt. None of this was her fault, and as for her poor children, it was certainly not fair that they should suffer because of what their father had done! In fact, thought Joanna even more angrily, this was all the fault of Elisha. If her husband hadn't heard Elisha speaking, he would never have gone to follow the holy men, and then he would have made money and left something for his family when he died. Yes, this was Elisha's fault, and he was going to have to do something about it! Joanna called her children and, holding their hands, she swept out of the house and went in search of Elisha.

Elisha was sitting peacefully in a clearing in the forest when Joanna marched up to him, a child on either side.

"You!" she said. "Look what you've done! My husband followed you, and now he's dead, and if I don't pay the money he owes by tomorrow, my children will be taken as payment instead!"

The holy man looked calmly up at her. "What

am I supposed to do about it?" he said. "Your husband followed God, not me."

"Yes, he believed in God, but he followed you," said Joanna.

"In that case, God and I will both help you," said Elisha. "What have you got in your house?"

"Nothing worth enough to pay what he owed," said Joanna. "The most valuable thing is a little jug of oil. The jug is worth nothing, and the oil is worth pennies."

"Listen," said Elisha. "Go home, but on your way, knock on every door you come to and ask to borrow an empty pot."

"An empty pot? I can't sell those!" said Joanna.

"You're not going to sell them – you're only borrowing them," said Elisha. "Get as many as you can, take them all home, lock yourselves into the house, and pour your oil into the pots."

"Pour my oil into the pots," repeated Joanna. "And what then?"

"That's all," said the holy man.

As Joanna stomped back along the road, her children had to keep running to catch up with her.

"What are we going to do, Mama?" they asked.

"Exactly what the man says, of course," said Joanna. "What else can we do?"

All the way home, whenever they passed a house, they knocked on the door and asked for an empty pot. Some people refused or sent them away, but most of them were happy to lend a container of some sort: bowls and jugs, cups and vases were added to their collection until Joanna and both the children were carrying them stacked high in their arms, and by the time they reached their house, a pile was teetering on Joanna's head too. They brought them all in, locked the door, and spread the containers out to cover the floor. Then Joanna fetched the little jug of oil.

"Mama, that jug won't fill even one of these pots," said the children.

"I know that," sighed Joanna, and she started to pour.

The bowl in front of her filled up with oil, right to the brim.

"Pass me another pot," said Joanna.

The children lined up to pass the empty pots along, and Joanna kept pouring. She poured the oil into shallow bowls and deep dishes; she poured it into cooking pots, teapots, coffee pots, and flower pots.

"Pass me another pot," said Joanna.

She poured the oil into cups and mugs and jugs and tubs. She poured it into a purple urn and a butter churn, a drinking flask and a tall green vase.

"Pass me another pot," said Joanna.

She poured the oil into a soup bowl, a salad bowl, and a mixing bowl; she poured it into a saucepan, a frying pan, and a (hopefully clean) bedpan.

"Pass me another pot," said Joanna.

"They're all full," said the children.

At once, the oil stopped pouring.

Joanna went back to Elisha, the tiny oil jug still dangling from her hand. He looked at her quizzically.

"How did it go?" he said.

"Every pot is full of oil," she replied. "If I sell it all, there will be enough to pay the debt and still plenty left over for us to live on."

"Sounds as if you'd better do that, then," said the holy man.

"You've saved my children," said Joanna. "I don't know how to thank you. It seems that my husband was right to follow you after all."

"Once again," said Elisha, "Your husband followed God, not me. And God has saved your children."

"Then I'll thank God," said Joanna. And she did, for the rest of their lives.

## Where does this story come from?

*You can find this story in 2 Kings 4:1–7. The widow is not given a name in the Bible, so I called her Joanna because it means "God has answered".*

## What does it make you think about?

*I think it's very interesting how God helped Joanna, not by just giving her the money she needed, but by using something she already had and something that others could give her. It's surprising how many miracles in the Bible start with things that already exist, and people willing to share them: there's the story about the boy who gave his packed lunch of five loaves and two fish to Jesus who then fed 5,000 people with it, or the stone jars full of water for washing that Jesus turned into wine. I think it means that God likes us to use the things we have and to join with the people around us, so that with his help, amazing things can happen.*

# Little Bee's Journey

In the land of Israel there lived a little girl whose name was Binah, but her friends called her Bee for short because she was as busy and as cheerful, as small and as sweet as a bee; and until the worst day of her life, nobody imagined that such a lovely girl could come to any harm.

But there was a war with Syria, and war is a time for terrible things. The soldiers came to Bee's village with swords, loud shouts, and fire. In the noise and confusion, when Bee's mother realized that they were going to be separated, she whispered to her daughter: "Whatever happens, don't give up. Never despair. Don't turn back or turn away. Our God will be with you there." Those words were the ones Bee kept in her heart as the Syrian soldiers carried her away, to a new country and a different life.

In Syria, Bee became a slave, owned by a rich and important family. Sir Naaman was the commander of the Syrian army and owned a big house with lots of land. Because Bee was so small, but also so busy and sensible, she wasn't sent out to work in the fields; instead she was given to Lady Naaman as a maid. Remembering her mother's words, Bee did her work with as many smiles as she could manage, and only dreamed of home when she was sure nobody was watching; but her new mistress often noticed the wistful look on her face, or heard her murmuring "never despair" under her breath as she swept the floor.

Sir and Lady Naaman quickly became fond of Bee. They liked her wildly inaccurate efforts to learn their language, the way she pulled faces to make the other children laugh, the way that she called the shawl she had brought with her "my little bit of Israel" and wrapped herself in it to say the prayers she remembered from home. And Bee became fond of the Naamans too: she liked the way that they hugged each other at the door when Sir Naaman came home, and the way that Lady Naaman slipped her an extra bit of breakfast when she felt especially homesick, and let her play with the cat. So when Sir Naaman became unwell, and Lady Naaman tiptoed around the house looking distracted, and there were whispered conversations in all the corners, Bee noticed and felt worried.

Over the next few weeks, the news spread between the servants of the household that Sir Naaman had leprosy, a horrible skin disease. There was no cure, they said, and it would only get worse; but Sir Naaman was trying to hide it from his soldiers, because the disease was catching, and if they knew about it then Sir Naaman could lose his job. Meanwhile, even Lady Naaman was trying not to get too close to her husband. There were no more hugs at the door, and Sir Naaman spent most of his time at his desk with his head in his hands.

Bee felt absolutely sure that there must be something she could do to help her master. As she went about her work, her mind buzzed through all the stories she had heard in Israel. When it landed on the right one, Bee stood straight up from washing the clothes and ran at once to Lady Naaman, surprising her as she was bringing a cup of tea up to her husband.

"Mistress, mistress!" she gasped, skidding to a stop in the doorway. "I know how Sir Naaman can get better! In my country, there was a prophet, a man of God who knew how to ask God for healing. If my master could only go there, he would be cured!"

From inside the room, Sir Naaman said, "Can that possibly be true? My doctors have said that this can never be cured."

"Don't give up!" said Bee. "Never despair. Don't turn back or turn away. My God can get you there."

So, Sir Naaman asked the king of Syria to write a letter, telling the king of Israel that he was coming in peace this time. He and Lady Naaman packed gold, clothes, and food for the journey into chariots drawn by strong horses – and in the one at the front perched Bee, wrapped in her little-bit-of-Israel shawl.

Very early one morning after days of journeying, the tired and dusty group arrived at the king of Israel's palace, and Sir Naaman solemnly handed over the letter from the king of Syria. They waited nervously in the courtyard as a servant delivered it. After a while they heard shouting and the slapping of bare feet along a tiled floor, and out came an angry little king in his nightshirt, waving the letter above his head.

"What do you mean by waking me up with this nonsense?" he squawked, marching toward Sir

Naaman. "The king of Syria has sent you here so that I can cure your leprosy? I can't cure leprosy! Nobody can do that! You're clearly trying to start a fight! Well, I won't have it! Guards, seize them!"

"I think the king of Syria might have misunderstood what I asked him to write in the letter," said Sir Naaman. "Better go home before we're captured."

"Home?!" said Bee. "Not now, after coming all this way! We must go and find the prophet ourselves. Don't give up! Never despair! Don't turn back or turn away. My God can get you there."

So, they galloped away from the guards and went on going until, at last, after a few wrong turns and asking lots of directions, they came to the house of the prophet Elisha. A servant hopped down from a chariot and knocked on the door. One of Elisha's servants answered it. They had a brief conversation, then the door closed again and Sir Naaman's servant turned back to him, looking a little nervous.

"Um... the prophet Elisha has a message for you. He says that you should go and wash in the River Jordan seven times, and you'll be healed."

Sir Naaman clenched his fists. He took a couple of deep breaths through his nose. The servant took a step backwards. And then Sir Naaman exploded.

"Oh, he does, does he? That's what he says, is it? So I've driven for days, dragging chariots full of gold and silver to pay for the best treatment from this amazing miracle worker, been shouted at by a king, chased by guards, and I've possibly started another war with Israel, just to be told to go and jump in a river? Does Mr Prophet Elisha perhaps think that we don't have rivers in Syria? Does he not know who I am? I thought he was going to come out and wave his hands around and perform wonders! Forget it. We're going back to Syria. Turn the chariots around!"

Bee couldn't take it any longer. She jumped down from her seat, stood in front of the chariots and horses, and yelled "STOP!" as loudly and as long as she could. Everyone went quiet and looked at her.

"Sir Naaman," said Bee, "look at yourself. Look at all this gold and silver you've brought. You would have been prepared to give all of that away just to be healed. You know that you would give up more than that if you could get well. Yet all you've been asked to do is have a wash. Why would you refuse to do a little thing, when you're prepared to give such big things?"

She pulled herself up to her full tiny height

and looked Sir Naaman in the eye. "Don't give up. Never despair. Don't turn back or turn away. My God will get you there."

"Fine," said Sir Naaman. "Fine. We'll go to the River Jordan."

So they did. Sir Naaman waded in, held his nose, and dipped under the water seven times – and when he came up for the seventh time, his skin was as soft and flawless as Bee's own.

The first thing he did was to give Lady Naaman a long, dripping hug. Then he told everyone to get the chariots ready.

"Are we going back to Syria now, sir?" asked the drivers.

"Back to Syria? Of course not!" said Sir Naaman. "We're going back to the prophet's house. He may not want any of my gifts, but I need to ask for one more thing from him."

"What's that?" asked Bee.

"I'm going to ask him to let me take a pile of earth so that I can stand on it to worship God," said Naaman. "My own little bit of Israel, Bee. I shall need it, because you see, I'm leaving my other little bit of Israel here."

"What do you mean?" said Bee, catching her breath.

"You, little Bee. You have given me a wonderful gift, and I am giving you your freedom. You are home now. Go and find your family."

"But... but I won't know where to go," faltered Bee, "or how to get there all by myself."

Sir Naaman squatted down so that his face was next to hers. "Don't give up, Bee," he said, "never despair. Don't turn back or turn away."

"My God will get me there?" said Bee.

"*Our* God will get you there," smiled Sir Naaman.

---

## Where does this story come from?

*This story is found in 2 Kings 5:1–19, part of the much longer story about the prophet Elisha and the kings of Israel. Elisha is the same holy man as in the story of Joanna and her pots. Naaman's little maid isn't named in the Bible, but I thought that Binah (pronounced Bee-NAH, Hebrew for "understanding") suited her.*

*We don't know as much about her as I've written in this story: for example, the Bible tells us that it was "Naaman's servants" who persuaded him to dip in the Jordan after he nearly went home, and I thought that could include Bee. Her freedom at the end is my wishful thinking, but considering how generous Naaman was prepared to be with his rewards, it's not impossible. The main message of the story is the same as it is in the Bible: it was the wisdom, faith, and courage of one little girl remembering her God's power that led to Naaman being healed.*

---

## What does it make you think about?

*This story is full of places: Israel and Syria, palaces and houses, and the River Jordan, a very special place in many Bible stories. The Israelites crossed the river on their way into the Promised Land, and Jesus was baptized there. It is still possible to visit the River Jordan today.*

*Naaman asked Elisha for some soil to take home so that he would have a little bit of Israel on which to stand and worship God, and I imagined that Bee used her shawl in the same way. Do you have a special place to go to be quiet, or somewhere (or something) that makes you think about God or others? Christians believe that people can talk to God anywhere at all, but sometimes having a place set aside can help.*

# Queen Esther, Nation Saver

## PART ONE

The crowded room was full of whispering, giggling, and the scent of perfumed oils. On every side of Esther, girls painted on eyeliner, brushed hair, dabbed lipstick, each awaiting her turn to go out on stage. But this was no ordinary beauty pageant. For a start, the contestants had not chosen to enter; they had been summoned to the palace, and nobody refuses a summons from the king. Secondly, the one judged most beautiful would win the dubious prize of becoming the new queen. Considering how quickly the last queen had been sent away merely for showing a bit of independence, thought Esther, it was surprising that the girls here weren't doing their best to appear the ugliest. People will do almost anything for riches and fame.

Even Esther had to admit though that the idea of being able to provide for her adoptive dad Mordecai in his old age was attractive. He had shared everything with her since the day her parents had died. Perhaps this competition, reluctant though she was to become queen, might at least be a chance to repay his kindness.

"Esther?" The door opened and an attendant peered around it, holding a list. "It's your moment." He held the door open for Esther to step before the king.

That evening, Esther met Mordecai at the palace gate. He opened his arms in greeting. "Esther! Never mind, my dear. Whatever the king thought, you're still the most beautiful girl in the world to me. Let's go and get dinner."

"I won," whispered Esther.

"You won?!" gasped Mordecai. "Then why the solemn face? Esther, this is wonderful!"

"Is it really?" Esther sighed. "I'll have to go and live in the palace, away from you. I'll have to be queen to a king who sent his last queen packing because she didn't follow one of his silly rules."

Esther wiped an anxious tear from her cheek with the palm of her hand.

Mordecai stopped, faced Esther, and put a hand on each of her shoulders. "Esther, I know things feel out of control and strange. Your life is changing very quickly. But one thing I always say is that there is a reason for every person to be where they are. This is your moment, my dear. Enjoy it!"

They walked on, Esther gazing blankly into the distance, Mordecai's hand still on her shoulder. She lifted her own hand to cover his. They left unspoken the thought that they had very little time left together as father and daughter. As they reached their little house, Mordecai turned to Esther again.

"I heard something while I was waiting for you by the palace gate," he said. "Two officials are plotting against the king. You must warn His Majesty of their plans the next time you see him. It will work well in your favour to show yourself on his side from the beginning."

Esther nodded.

"Oh, and one more thing," said Mordecai, "it might be as well not to let the king know too much about you. Where you come from, your Jewish family, that kind of thing."

"Why not?" said Esther, surprised.

"History, Esther, history," Mordecai sighed. "The old story. One kingdom invades another kingdom, and they live together with a fragile peace. We are allowed to be here, Esther, but not everybody likes us. We're different. It's just best not to make a big song and dance about it."

"You've always given me good advice, Mordecai," smiled Esther.

"And you've almost always taken it," grinned Mordecai, ruffling her hair.

The wedding and the coronation took place on the same day. Esther, crowned queen, was cheered by crowds as she took her place next to her new husband. During the party that followed, she took her chance to tell the king about what Mordecai had heard at the gate. The king was so pleased with her that as soon as he had ordered the two traitors to be executed, he wrote Mordecai's name into a big book of "Deeds That Have Pleased The King".

And that was as much as Esther saw of her husband. The following morning, one of the stewards, Atak, took her through the many, many rules about living in the palace.

"Nobody may enter the king's presence without being called," he told her sternly. "Not even you, Your Majesty. If you find yourself within sight of the king, even accidentally, you will be sentenced to death unless he points his sceptre at you to show that he approves of your being there."

Esther shuddered. What kind of a life was this?

"Does everybody always do everything the king commands?" she asked.

"Of course, Your Majesty. Right now, for example, he has commanded everybody to bow down before his newly appointed right-hand man, Haman," said Atak. "And just look out of your window!"

Esther looked down into the courtyard, where sure enough, a finely dressed man was parading around while everyone he passed bowed down to the ground. Eventually he left through the palace gate, with even the servants attending him continuing to bow as they walked. As they passed through the gate, Esther could see some sort of commotion taking place on the other side – someone had refused to bow, and there was a lot of shouting. She drew her head back in wearily.

"The king is my husband," she said. "What if I need to tell him something?"

"You just have to wait," answered Atak kindly. "Don't worry. I'm sure he'll want to see you often enough."

Despite these words, the weeks went by without a call from the king. Esther didn't mind very much; since she had only ever spoken to her husband twice, she didn't miss him. She did, however, miss Mordecai a great deal. After much begging, Atak – her only friend in this huge, lonely, boring palace – agreed to go to see how Mordecai was getting on. When he returned, his face looked pale.

"Mordecai is sitting at the palace gate dressed in sackcloth and ashes," he said, "and he refuses to move. Something must be wrong."

Esther didn't lose a moment. Forgetting that she was supposed to stay quietly inside, she flew down the stairs, across the courtyard, and into Mordecai's astonished arms.

"Esther, my dear! At last!" he cried.

"Mordecai, what is this? What do you need? Why are you wearing sackcloth as if someone has died? Should I send you clothes, or money?" asked Esther.

"It's not just me, but all our people who need your help, my dear," explained Mordecai. "You see, that man Haman, the king's right-hand man to whom everyone is supposed to bow down…"

"Yes, I remember him," said Esther. "What a stuck-up brute he is. I saw the fuss he made when someone refused to bow as he left the palace a few weeks ago."

"That was me," said Mordecai. "I refused."

"Mordecai! But why? I mean, he's horrible, but why risk your life over such a small thing?"

"Esther, my dear, as I told Haman to his silly, proud face, we Jews only ever bow to one person, and that is the God we worship. It's written in our law."

Esther dropped her head into her hands. "Oh, Mordecai! If this gets back to the king…"

"It's worse than that, Esther. Now listen – we don't have long. I can already see that steward of yours coming to fetch you. This is what has happened: Haman has decided, not just to kill me, but to kill all of us. All your people, Esther, and you too – if he knew that you were one of us. He has done this by tricking the king into signing a command. You have to stop that command being carried out, Esther. You must go to the king and tell him that the command he has signed destroys you and your family."

"If only it were that simple!" moaned Esther. "I'm not allowed to just go and see the king – on pain of death, I must wait until he calls me. It's been…" she counted on her fingers, "a month, with no call."

"Esther." Mordecai reached out both his hands and placed them, in that familiar gesture, on her shoulders. "You must gather up your courage and go anyway. This is the reason, my dear, why you were made queen – you and nobody else can save us. You, exactly who you are and where you are in this instant, you are our one hope. This is your moment."

Esther swallowed. She took a deep breath. Atak hovered behind her, clearing his throat. Esther stood and clasped Mordecai's hand.

"This might be the last time I see you," she said, looking deep into his eyes, willing him to catch her meaning. "I'm going now."

* * *

Esther strode across the courtyard, her skirts swirling up dust, her arms swinging purposefully. Beside her, Atak scurried to keep up, doing his best to hold her back.

"But, Your Majesty... you remember... I told you, the rule says... this is just the kind of thing that the last queen... please, wait! You could die..."

As Esther reached the door of the throne room, Atak fell back reluctantly, not willing to risk being seen himself. Esther pushed the heavy door open and stepped into silence.

She stood, chest heaving, staring down the long gleaming hall to the throne where the king sat. He had leaped back at the sound of the door, and both hands gripped the arms of the throne. The look of fearful surprise on his face turned to anger, then puzzlement. He frowned at her. Still she did not speak. She allowed her breathing to quiet, and relaxed her shoulders, holding his gaze. He narrowed his eyes, tilting his head to the side. Then he raised his sceptre and pointed it at her.

"Esther, my queen, my love," he smiled. "You made me jump. Come over here and tell me what you desire."

Feeling almost faint with relief, Esther made the long walk to the throne.

"Your Majesty, I've been missing you," she said, "and I know how busy you are, but I would like to invite you and your right-hand man Haman to a feast. A chance for you both to relax."

"What a sweet idea! Certainly, my love. We'll come to your quarters tomorrow night," said the king.

Esther bowed her head, backed toward the door, and slipped out, beckoning an astonished Atak as she closed the door behind her.

"We have a feast to prepare, Atak. Get started," she said. "I have a few other things to deal with."

---

## Where does this story come from?

*Esther has her very own book in the Bible. Find out more about it after part two!*

---

## What does it make you think about?

*What do you think will happen next?*

# Queen Esther, Nation Saver

## PART TWO

Esther set off in search of Haman. He was never hard to find. His loud, sneering tones could be heard all over the palace, and he loved to be seen, so he tended to conduct his meetings in the open air. Today she followed his boasting laugh to a corner of the garden, where he was sitting with his wife and several servants and advisors. Checking that her face didn't show her disgust too clearly, Esther approached, gave her invitation as quickly as possible, and withdrew. As she walked away, Haman started his boasting again.

"You see how great I am? Even the queen invites me, personally, to come to dinner with her and the king! I'm the best!"

"Indeed you are, dear," simpered his wife.

"Ugh," thought Esther, quickening her pace.

"That dreadful Mordecai at the gate is the only thing that spoils it for me," Haman went on. Esther paused, looked over her shoulder to check that nobody was looking, and slipped behind a tree. "Every day I have to walk past him, in his disgusting sackcloth, and he never bows, even though he knows how I'm punishing him and his savage people."

"Then why not deal with him at once, dear? Don't wait for this command of the king's to go through," advised Haman's wife. "Execute the man straight away and put your mind at rest. Nobody will say no to you."

"You're nearly as clever as me, my dear," replied Haman. "But I'll go one better than that. I won't just kill him. I'll kill him on the biggest gallows anyone has ever seen. He'll be strung up so high that the whole country will be able to see it. Servants! Go and build me gallows like that, right in my front garden!"

The servants scampered off, and Esther,

feeling sick, crawled from behind the tree and out of the garden, using the bushes as a cover.

That night, Esther couldn't sleep, and her half-conscious nightmares were full of giant gallows, pointing sceptres, and Haman's sneering laugh. At last she got up from her bed and went to the window for some fresh air. Beneath the window, two servants were talking.

"The king can't sleep again," whispered the first servant. "He keeps waking and crying out. I don't know what to do for him."

"Well, don't ask me," said the second one. "I was on duty last night, and nothing I did was any help. He didn't sleep a wink all night."

Esther, suddenly inspired, leaned out of the window. "You two," she said. "You know that big book of 'Deeds That Have Pleased The King' that's in the palace library? Why don't you try reading it to him? Hearing about the support and love of his citizens will help to calm his fears – and failing that, such a big book is bound to send him to sleep eventually."

"That's a great idea! Thanks! I'll go and get it," said the first servant.

"One more thing," said Esther. "Start with the most recent entry and read it backwards. The king needs to know that even in the last few days, his people have been protecting and praising him."

Then she closed the window and went smiling to bed.

\* \* \*

Early the next morning, Esther woke up to the sound of shouting in the courtyard. Looking out of her window, she saw the king in his nightgown, clutching the book of Deeds, storming out of his quarters with several anxious servants surrounding him.

"How is it possible that nothing was done to reward him?" raged the king. "I need an official, now! Who's about? Ah, Haman!" for the man himself was just coming in through the gate.

Haman strode purposefully over.

"Your Majesty, I want to tell you about my plan to execute..."

"Never mind that just now, Haman. Tell me: what should be done for a man the king wishes to honour and reward? A subject who is truly faithful and loyal and should be held up as an example – what should I do for him?"

Haman puffed out his chest and said importantly, "Your Majesty knows he is asking the right person." Then he winked.

"He thinks the king's talking about him!"

Esther realized, stifling a laugh.

"For such a man, Your Majesty, only the best treatment! Let him ride the king's finest horse. Let him be led around the city by a well-known representative of the palace, someone high up in government, perhaps. And so that everybody sees, let that person shout at the top of their voice: 'THIS IS WHAT THE KING DOES FOR A REALLY GREAT MAN!'"

"Excellent suggestion, Haman. You may..." – here Haman pulled himself up even taller and lifted his chin – "be that representative. The man you're rewarding is Mordecai, who months ago reported a plot against my life. Go and get my finest horse and see that it's done exactly as you described."

Haman deflated like a punctured football as the king turned to go back inside, and Esther had to stuff her sleeve into her mouth to stop her laughter.

A little while later, Atak came into the room and looked at Esther curiously. "Haman is leading Mordecai around the city on a horse, shouting about what a great man he is, in between sobbing and wiping his nose on his sleeve. He has a face like a whipped camel. That wouldn't have anything to do with you, would it, Your Majesty?"

"I've been sitting here all morning," said Esther innocently, her mouth twitching.

Atak raised an eyebrow, but his eyes were laughing. "This evening's feast is nearly ready, Your Majesty," he said with a bow.

As the sun went down, Esther sat at a table laden with food, ready to entertain her guests. When Haman and the king arrived, they found a feast spread out, servants ready to hand them tall cups of wine, and candles twinkling in the twilight at every window. The king relaxed into his chair with a sigh.

"This was a wonderful idea, my darling," he said to Esther. "Just what I needed. Let me do something for you, too. Tell me anything you want in my kingdom, and it's yours."

Esther glanced at Haman, who was admiring himself reflected in his golden wine cup, smiling like toothache. She thought of Mordecai, wearing sackcloth at the gate and waiting to die. She pictured the giant gallows set up for him, and imagined the horror if Haman's plan worked and all her people were slaughtered too. The fact that she might be about to die seemed small in comparison, and she heard Mordecai's voice saying, "This is your moment." So, she looked the king in the eyes.

"Save my life," she said.

"What?" The king jumped and looked around fearfully. "Are we in danger?"

"Not you, but I am," said Esther. "Somebody has tricked you into signing a command that will take my life, and my whole family, and all my people."

Haman froze in the middle of a sip of wine and sat like a statue with the cup to his lips.

"What?! What traitor has plotted to kill the queen?!" gasped the king, clutching at the neck of his cloak.

"He is sharing this table with us," said Esther. "It's Haman."

The king leaped up, gibbering with rage, then bolted for the courtyard shouting, "Guards! Guards!"

Haman, turning white, threw himself to the floor at Esther's feet, tweaking the bottom of her dress, and making little puppyish whimpering noises.

"Oh, great queen, spare my life! I'll be your best friend! I'll let you tell everyone that you know me!" he whined up at her, hugging her knees.

The king crashed back into the room with two soldiers. "Look! He's trying to hurt her even now, in front of me! How quickly can we get rid of this dreadful traitor?"

The soldiers looked at each other.

"He's got his very own giant gallows," one said, "in his front garden. He had it built this morning for Mordecai."

"For Mordecai?!" spluttered the king. "He was going to hang Mordecai, the one who I rewarded when I found his name in my book of Deeds – that Mordecai?!"

"The very same," said the guard.

"Then hang him in his own front garden! At once!" roared the king.

Once the guards had gone, dragging Haman between them, the king sank into a chair and put his head in his hands.

"I suppose I need a new right-hand man," he said.

"May I make one more suggestion?" said Esther.

So Mordecai was brought in from the palace gate, dressed in fine clothes, and given Haman's signet ring with the seal that showed a command came from the king. The first thing he did with it was to take back the command about killing all the Jewish people. The people had a big party to celebrate, and at Esther's command, they still do every year.

As for Esther, with Mordecai there in the palace and a king who could at last trust his nearest and dearest, she lived happily ever after.

## Where does this story come from?

*Esther, like Ruth, has her very own book named after her. Jewish people today still celebrate a festival called Purim, the one that Esther ordered at the end of this story. Sometimes they tell the story as a kind of pantomime, called a Purim Spiel; and when they read out the story in the synagogue, they make a loud noise with whistles and rattles to blot out Haman's name every time he is mentioned. They celebrate the day with gifts and sweet treats.*

*By the way, the steward's name was really Hathach, but I have spelt it Atak because it looked so similar to Haman. Too many unfamiliar names can be confusing! That's why I also haven't named the king, who is called Ahasuerus or Xerxes.*

## What does it make you think about?

*Esther found herself in a dangerous and unhappy position, but Mordecai told her that perhaps this was exactly where she needed to be: the only person who could save a whole nation. His words in the Bible are: "Who knows whether you have not come to the kingdom for such a time as this?" (Esther 4:14)*

*Think of all the different places and situations you find yourself in. Could there be a special job in one of them that only you can do?*

# Martha and Mary

There were once two sisters who were as different from one another as the dry land is from the sea. Martha, the elder, was tall and angular; Mary, the younger, was petite and soft-skinned. Martha never sat still; all day long, her busy feet hurried about, and her hands, when they weren't busy cooking, cleaning, or sewing, fiddled and jumped as if of their own accord. Mary, on the other hand, was capable of sitting so still that she blended into her background like a tawny owl in a tree, her big dark eyes the only movement, so that you might walk past and not notice her at all.

Martha loved people. She loved to fill the house with guests, squeezed as tightly as possible around the table; she loved the bustling streets and the crowds in the town on market day. Mary preferred her people one at a time or not at all. She could spend hours alone, just thinking.

Anyone who knew the sisters would shake their heads and fondly wonder how on earth such different people could live together and get along, let alone be related to each other; but in fact, Martha and Mary had plenty in common. They both loved their little house in Bethany. They both missed their parents, who had died very young. And they both adored their younger brother, Lazarus. Lazarus had a condition that caused him long bouts of illness, so that he couldn't always move about or go to work, which meant that the two sisters had cared for him since he was a child: Martha by doing all his cooking and cleaning and making up his medicines, Mary by sitting by his bedside in the bad times, reading to him or singing soothing songs.

Martha and Mary had something else in common too. They had both met Jesus and become his very best friends.

It happened because of Martha, of course; she was already friends with several of Jesus' disciples, and when they started talking about this man they were following, she just had to meet him, so she invited them all over for dinner. After that, Jesus and anybody he happened to have with him would always come to stay whenever they passed through Bethany. What wonderful times they had! Lazarus, when he was well enough, would lie at the table and join in the discussion; Martha would busy herself in the kitchen and bring out fabulous feasts; and Mary would take any opportunity to draw a guest into a quiet corner with her and listen intently to their story. She loved it best of all when that guest was Jesus.

Of course, sometimes the sisters' differences caused squabbles. On one occasion, Mary was sitting listening to Jesus when everything went wrong for Martha in the kitchen. A pot boiled over on the fire; Martha ran to rescue it but tripped over the cat and dropped the basket of bread she was holding and, at the same time, Lazarus called her urgently from his room. Martha marched over to Mary and Jesus, brandishing a spoon.

"Lord, don't you care that I'm doing all the work here? Tell my lazy sister to get up and help me!"

Jesus looked fondly from typical Mary to typical Martha. "Martha, you're worried about so many things all at once," he said. "Not all of them are necessary, you know. Mary's made a good choice about how to spend her time, and I'm not going to take that away from her."

Martha stood there fizzing for a moment, then took a deep breath, clenched her teeth, and marched off to sort out the mess.

Then, one winter, things began to change. More people had heard about Jesus and some of them didn't like what they heard. There was a plot to arrest him, and so Martha and Mary saw much less of him and his disciples for a while as they journeyed elsewhere. They would have missed him even more than they did, had it not been for something else taking up most of their time: Lazarus was unwell again, and this time it was much worse than before and went on for much longer. Martha, of course, was busy, trying to cook foods that would tempt and strengthen him, finding medicines that would help him, asking doctor after doctor whether anything more could be done. Several times she tried to find Jesus, and when she couldn't, she wrote him a letter asking him to come. Mary stayed at home, sitting by her brother's bed, holding his hand, and praying; and so it was Mary who was with Lazarus when he died.

The two sisters were full of grief. After the funeral, even Martha didn't want to be with crowds of people. Even Mary didn't want to spend too long alone. They held each other, and cried; and together they wondered where their friend Jesus was. Why hadn't he come when they needed him?

A few days later, a rumour spread in Bethany that Jesus had been seen on the road, heading their way. At once Martha jumped up, put on her cloak, and went to the door.

"Aren't you coming, Mary?" she asked, but Mary only shrank further back into her corner. Martha shook her head in exasperation and marched out. She didn't have time for Mary's quiet stillness now; she was going to give Jesus a piece of her mind.

"If you had been here, our brother would still be alive!" They were the first words out of her mouth when she spotted Jesus on the road, before she had even stopped walking toward him. She stood, out of breath, clenching her jaw, and swallowing against the rising tears.

"I know you," she whispered. "I know that whatever you ask from God, he will give to you. Didn't you want to be here?"

Jesus looked steadily at his friend. "Your brother will rise again."

"Yes, yes, I know that we will all rise and live together one day," said Martha. "You talk about it often. It's called the resurrection. But..."

"Martha, I am the resurrection," said Jesus. "I am

life itself. Whoever believes in me lives, even when they die. Do you believe me?"

Martha looked at Jesus and felt herself being filled up, from her feet to her head, with a sure knowledge and peace. Her fidgeting hands dropped still by her sides.

"I believe you," she said. "I believe that you are the Christ – the Son of God – the promised one."

Jesus smiled. "Where's your sister?" he said.

Martha ran to fetch Mary, who came as soon as she heard that Jesus had asked for her. But when she saw Jesus, she couldn't contain herself, and threw her arms around him with exactly the words that Martha had said: "Lord, if you had been here, our brother would still be alive."

Jesus looked at her tearful face and started to cry. "Where is he?" he asked, and together they walked to Lazarus's tomb, a cave in a rock with a stone sealed across the front. As they walked, a crowd that had gathered on the road followed them.

"Take away the stone," said Jesus, his face covered in tears.

Martha, ever practical even in her grief, wrinkled her nose. "Lord, it will smell. It's been four days since the funeral," she explained.

Jesus turned to her with that intent look of his.

"What did you say about believing in me?" he asked.

Martha nodded. "All right. Roll away the stone," she said to the gathering crowd, and when they hesitated, she said it more loudly: "Roll it away!"

Once the tomb was open, Jesus held out his hands and prayed. Then he shouted, "Lazarus, come out!"

There was silence. Mary reached for Martha's hand. Nobody breathed. Then a rustling sound came from inside the cave; then, footsteps. Martha gripped her sister's hand as a figure emerged from the tomb.

He was still wrapped in grave clothes. He had a cloth over his head. He was stumbling and a bit confused – but he was Lazarus, their brother. And he was alive.

Jesus smiled at his friends. "Untie him," he said, "and take him home."

Several weeks later, they all sat around the table again: Jesus, his disciples, and Lazarus, in his old place. Martha, of course, was serving them delicious food she'd spent all day preparing; but her shoulders were relaxed and she was taking time to chat to each guest as she handed them their plate. Mary, of course, was sitting by each person one at a time; but she was helping. She had offered to do the job of washing each guest's feet as they arrived, because she had a secret plan. When she came to Jesus, she brought out a bottle of very expensive, sweet-smelling oil and, instead of water, poured it over his feet as a wordless sign of her gratitude and love.

The scent spread around the whole room, and people looked up to see what it was, all eyes eventually alighting on Mary. Judas, one of the disciples, rolled his eyes.

"Don't you know what that costs?" he asked. "Couldn't the money have been given to the poor?"

Mary felt a moment of doubt. But Jesus shook his head.

"Leave her be," he told Judas. "Mary will always be ready to help the poor, but she won't always have me."

Mary, kneeling at his feet, looked up and waited. Martha, across the room, stopped and put down a pile of dishes. Everyone was listening. But Jesus didn't say more; he simply looked over at typical Martha by the table, looked down at typical Mary at his feet, and smiled fondly at both his friends.

## Where does this story come from?

*Martha and Mary appear in several episodes in the gospels. The first part of their story can be found i n Luke 10:38–42, and the rest in John, chapter 11 and the beginning of chapter 12.*

*We don't know what Lazarus's illness was, or whether he was ill for a long time as I've imagined here. Some people think he might have been, since Martha seems to be the head of the household, and that would usually have been the man; and others think, because of similar stories and names in other places in the Bible, that his illness may have been leprosy – like Sir Naaman in the story about Little Bee – but we don't know for sure.*

## What does it make you think about?

*What I like about Martha and Mary is the way that their different personalities shine through all the stories about them, but what becomes clear is that neither of them has the "right" way to think or act; they are both important at different parts of the story, and it is obvious that Jesus loved them both exactly as they were and treated them individually according to their differences. Martha's strong faith in action and Mary's heartfelt devotion make them both equally important people to remember.*

# Mary Cleopas

"The first time I saw him was at our wedding," Mary said to her husband Cleopas as they walked along. "Do you remember? He was just your nephew then. Just Joseph's boy. And then the wine ran out."

"His mother had a little chat with him in the corner," said Cleopas, taking up the well-worn story, "and the next thing we knew, all the servants were filling those vast stone jars with water instead of serving our guests. I was really angry for a bit, wasn't I? Trying to work out what was going on. But good old Ben came racing over with a glass of wine – 'Where did you find this?!' he says, 'Usually people have the good wine first and save the best for when everyone's drunk – what are you doing bringing the good stuff out now?!'"

"Best wine I've ever tasted, before or since," agreed Mary, automatically finishing the story the way they always did; but her mind was already wandering, remembering how that man, the one who had changed water into wine, had hung on a cross just two days ago. How she had watched helplessly, holding his mother's hand tight in hers, while a soldier pushed a spear into his body to check that he was dead, and what looked like water and red wine had come pouring out.

"You didn't know what kind of a family you were marrying into," said Cleopas, and his attempt at a light-hearted comment fell flat at their feet like another stone along the path.

They walked in silence for a little while, and Mary looked down and watched their feet: trudge, trudge, trudge, every step taking her away from Jerusalem, away from the others who knew how she felt. How could she explain to Cleopas so that he would understand what she had seen?

"Remember the time on that hillside," she began, "when he taught past three mealtimes and nobody had brought any food?"

"That little boy gave him a few bread rolls and a couple of fish," said Cleopas.

"Yes," continued Mary, "and he lifted the bread up and said a blessing, thanking God for it, and then he broke it..."

"And he kept on breaking it! Over and over again! Must have been about 5,000 there that day, and they all got something to eat," said Cleopas.

"And we knew he was special, Cleopas. We knew, didn't we? Anybody could see it."

"Well," said Cleopas, "nobody's saying he wasn't special, Mary. Nobody could say that, could they? He was just perhaps not as special as we thought."

Mary fell silent again, remembering that morning, when she and the other women had gone to the tomb, how they had walked along before the sun rose, wondering how they were ever going to move the huge stone that sealed the entrance to where he lay so that they could anoint his body with the myrrh they had brought. But when they arrived in the garden, the tomb was broken open like a fresh loaf, and they saw... they saw...

"Cleopas," she said, "we really did see it. The shining didn't come from the sun. The sun hadn't yet come up. We really did see an angel, and it really did tell us to go back to Jerusalem, and I honestly think we should…"

"Mary," said Cleopas patiently, "you were overtired, and you still are. Look at you! You haven't slept in three days. Four exhausted, grieving women in the dark are bound to start seeing and hearing things. Anyway, the others went and delivered whatever message it was they thought they'd been given, so you can put your conscience at rest. We'll be home soon, and you can go to bed, and tomorrow everything will make a little bit more sense, my dear."

Mary looked back down at their feet. Trudge, trudge, trudge away. Maybe her husband was right and it was all over. Maybe it really was very unlikely that God would choose four exhausted women to pass on any sort of important message. But then again… she had another memory, of standing on the edge of all the men listening to Jesus telling stories. When he caught her eye, he started a new one.

"A woman was making bread," he had said, "and she hid yeast in the flour. Nobody could see it was there! But the dough started to rise. The kingdom of heaven is like that…"

Mary took another breath to try talking to Cleopas again, but out of the corner of her eye, she noticed an extra pair of feet. Somebody had joined them on the road. She looked over at the stranger. He walked with a staff and a hat, like somebody whose journey had taken them through the hottest part of the day without a rest. He gave her a little smile.

"What are you talking about?" he asked. "You seem sad."

They all stopped for a moment, facing each other across the road. Mary took another breath, but Cleopas started talking first.

"You must be the only person around here who doesn't know what's happened in Jerusalem these last few days," he said.

"So, tell me," said the stranger.

"Jesus of Nazareth has been crucified," said Cleopas, and when the stranger looked blank, he went on. "He was an extraordinary prophet who performed miracles..." At this, Mary raised her eyebrows and gave him a stare.

"Well, yes, some of us had hoped that he was more than that," said Cleopas, "that he was the Messiah, the one to save God's people. But now that he's dead..." Mary coughed. "Well, yes, some of our women went to his tomb this morning and it was empty, and they even came back saying they'd seen some sort of vision of an angel, but... well. They didn't see him. And you know how women can get when they're together."

"Odd," said the stranger, "I thought the prophets said that something just like this would happen to the Messiah. Hasn't anybody mentioned that?"

They started to walk again, together, along the road away from Jerusalem, while the stranger began to talk about Moses and the prophets and the Messiah. Mary looked down. The light of the setting sun turned the sandy road breadcrumb gold, and she stepped along it, so tired that she could barely put one foot in front of the other. Still, she let the words drop into her mind and heart to think about later. Beneath the exhaustion and the grief, she sensed another feeling. Something like excitement, perhaps? Or joy? But that didn't make sense.

With relief, Mary recognized their village, their street, and then their front door. She turned to the stranger, suddenly not wanting to lose him.

"Come in and finish telling us all this over dinner," she said. "I baked some bread before I left, and we can have it with soup. The sun is going down – you won't get much further tonight – stay with us."

"Well, thank you," smiled the stranger.

The three of them went inside, and Mary lit

the fire under the soup pot, laid the table, and fetched the bread. Once they had all washed and were sitting together at the table, the stranger reached out and picked up Mary's loaf, the dough that she had worked yeast into and left to rise and then baked. He lifted it up above the plate, said a prayer of blessing to thank God, and broke it. Mary looked up, and her mouth fell open as she suddenly recognized Jesus. Then he vanished.

Mary looked at Cleopas. His mouth was hanging open too.

"That was Jesus!" she said.

"I know!" he said.

"I knew it! Didn't you know it? Did you get that feeling on the road, like something burning in you, like excitement or joy?"

"I did. You're right. I did feel it," said Cleopas.

"Cleopas, you know what this means, don't you?" Mary was already on her feet, putting their meal into a basket. "We have to go back to Jerusalem! We have to tell everybody! Jesus is alive, and he really is the Messiah, and I really did see an angel, and..."

"All right, all right!" laughed Cleopas. "You're right, and you were right all along. But are you sure you want to leave straight away? You're not too tired?"

"Tired? Not even a little bit! In fact," she said as they hurried out of the door, "it feels as if the day is just beginning."

---

## Where does this story come from?

*Mary Cleopas is given her full name only once in the list of women who were at the cross in the Gospel of John. (Sometimes it is spelled "Clopas".) But she is listed with just the name "Mary" among the women at the cross and at the tomb in the other gospels too; and it is likely that she was the unnamed disciple on the road to Emmaus in Luke 24:13–35, since her second name shows that she was married to Cleopas, the one who is named. When the gospels were written, women were often not named as witnesses because it was thought that they were unreliable, which is why it's wonderful that it was women who first saw the empty tomb and spread the good news of Jesus' resurrection to the other disciples.*

---

## What does it make you think about?

*If the other disciple on the road to Emmaus really was Mary Cleopas, she must have been wondering whether to believe her own eyes. In just three days she had watched Jesus die, found the tomb empty, and seen an angel saying that he was alive again; and now she was walking home as if it was all over.*

*Have you ever felt absolutely sure about something? What kind of things can you feel sure about, and how does that feel? What kind of things are you less certain about? In the Bible, after the disciples realized that the stranger had been Jesus all along, they said to each other, "Didn't we feel our hearts burning within us while he talked?" I think that when it comes to faith, everyone has times of certainty and times of doubt, but Christians believe that the truth about Jesus is something about which we can always feel sure.*

# Rhoda

There was once a little girl called Rhoda who spent so much of her time in a daydream that she did all sorts of silly things. She worked as a servant girl in a house which belonged to a lady called Mary and her son, whose name was Mark. Mary and Mark were very fond of Rhoda, but rather exasperated by her as well.

"Silly Rhoda!" Mary would say, when Rhoda forgot to take the bread out of the oven and burnt it.

"Silly Rhoda!" Mark would sigh, when Rhoda accidentally sewed the neck of his shirt closed while trying to patch it.

And then there was the time that Rhoda lost the keys for a week and then eventually found them in the hen house. "Oh, Rhoda!" they said.

Mary and Mark were Christians, and sometimes the church had to meet secretly in their house, because King Herod was arresting and occasionally killing people who admitted that they followed Jesus.

Rhoda loved to listen to their secret meetings and daydream about the stories they told, imagining that she too had met Jesus and seen him do the amazing things they talked about.

One of the best storytellers that came to Mary and Mark's house was Peter, who had been one of Jesus' disciples. Whenever he came to stay, Rhoda would leave her work and creep into the meeting to hear him.

But one day, King Herod arrested Peter and put him in prison for telling people about Jesus. It was a few days before the Passover festival, the day of the year when Jesus had died on the cross, and Mary and Mark suspected that Herod wanted to make an example of Peter by doing the same thing to him on the same day. So, they invited all the other Christians to their house and together they prayed urgently for Peter.

With so many people in the house, there was lots of extra work to do, but Rhoda's mind was on Peter. While everyone else prayed, she daydreamed about how God might rescue him. And while she daydreamed, she made mistakes.

"Silly Rhoda!" Mary said, when Rhoda left the cheese in the sun and it melted.

"Silly Rhoda!" Mark sighed, when Rhoda tried to change the sheets on a bed that still had a guest sleeping in it.

And then there was the moment that Rhoda walked in carefully balancing a large plate piled high with figs and raisins – and swatted a fly at the same time. "Oh, Rhoda!" they all said, picking sticky dried fruit out of their hair.

That evening, while everybody was praying together in the sitting room, there was a knock at the door. Rhoda went to answer it, her heart beating fast in case it was Herod's soldiers. What if they had found out where the church was meeting?

She pressed her ear to the inside of the door and called out in a thin, trembling voice: "Who is it?"

"Rhoda? Is that you? It's Peter!"

"It's Peter!" shrieked Rhoda, and flew back down the hall, crashing into the room where everyone was praying, and tripping over the carpet.

"Silly Rhoda!" said Mary. "Who was at the door?"

"It's Peter!" said Rhoda, picking herself up.

"Silly Rhoda!" said Mark. "Of course it isn't Peter. He's in prison."

"I know, but it really is him!" insisted Rhoda. "I wouldn't mistake his voice for anyone else. God must have rescued him from prison."

"Where is he, then, Rhoda?" laughed Mark.

At that moment, there was another knock at the door, and Rhoda gasped.

"Oh! I forgot to let him in!"

"Oh, Rhoda!" said everybody.

Rhoda raced back to the door and flung it open. There on the other side stood Peter, who swept her up in a big hug.

"Where is everyone?" he asked.

"They're in the sitting room, praying for you," said Rhoda. "How did God do it? How did he set you free?"

"It was an angel," said Peter. "I thought I was dreaming when this huge, shining person came into the prison cell, undid my shackles, and led me out straight past the guards. In fact, I still thought that I would wake up and find myself back in prison until the moment the angel left me in the street! Then I thought I'd better come here."

Rhoda led Peter into the sitting room, where he told the story again to the amazed group, finishing with "... and if Rhoda hadn't come back to open the door, I might be standing out there still!"

"Silly Rhoda!" they laughed.

"Actually, no. It's you who are silly," said Rhoda. They all turned to look at her.

"You're silly for not believing me that it was Peter," she continued. "You're silly for sitting in here praying that God would help Peter, but then thinking that it couldn't be him outside the door! You always say that God can do miracles, but then you didn't believe it when he did one!"

"Clever Rhoda," said Mary, "You're right."

"Well done, Rhoda!" said Mark. "You had more faith than the rest of us put together."

Peter just smiled, thinking of how Rhoda always crept in to listen when he told his stories, and how her face shone when he talked about his friend Jesus.

"Dear Rhoda!" he said.

---

## Where does this story come from?

*This story can be found in Acts 12:6–17. Unusually for a girl mentioned only once in the Bible, Rhoda is actually given her name, showing that she made quite an impression. Perhaps Luke (the writer of the book of Acts) was as fond of her as Peter was.*

---

## What does it make you think about?

*The story of Rhoda makes me think about something that Jesus once said: that to enter the kingdom of heaven, everybody should become like children (Matthew 18:2–4). We don't know exactly how old Rhoda was, but her faith is perfectly child-like. In contrast with the adults around her, she sees no reason to doubt the miracles that she has been told are true. What kinds of things do you find easy to believe, and what is more difficult? Do you think that people grow out of believing certain things?*

# Lydia

When Lydia was a little girl, she had one dream, one ambition. It was probably not one that she shared with any other little girl living at that time, and I don't suppose that any girls living today share Lydia's dream either. But for Lydia it was all-consuming, the one idea that filled up her days and decorated her nights.

Lydia dreamed of purple.

Lydia lived in Thyatira with her father and they worked in the fabric trade, making purple dye out of the roots of a plant called madder. They called it purple, but the shade made by the madder root was really more of a dark, muddy red. Thyatira was famous for producing that tone of dye, and Lydia, along with her brothers and sisters, learned the business by watching and helping her father to buy the plants, making the madder dye, and dyeing the cloth to sell.

But Lydia dreamed of true purple. She saw it once, on the hem of a rich man's toga as he gave a speech from the steps of a temple. Lydia didn't hear a word the man said – she just stared at the glorious purple of the hem contrasting with the crisp white cloth. Afterwards she asked her father, "How do they make true purple?"

Her father frowned. "It comes from a certain type of sea-snail," he said. "It takes thousands of the snails to make even a small cup of the dye: that's why it's so expensive and so rare. And that's why madder purple is such good business. It's still expensive, but much more affordable for our customers."

From then on, though, Lydia dreamed of true purple. She wandered in the fields and picked flowers that came close to the right shade, but they dried and faded. She lingered by the temple where she had seen the purple on a toga, hoping for another glimpse; she heard lots of talk about religion, but she never saw the man who was important enough to wear purple. As she pegged out the madder-dyed cloth to dry, she looked at the sun shining through it and could almost imagine that it glowed with the purple of her dreams, but when she folded it, it turned back to dull red.

One day, by the temple steps again, Lydia overheard a conversation between some men who were arguing that their Greek gods were the right ones to follow, and another group who were talking about one true God. Lydia, who had grown up with the Greek gods, was curious.

"Perhaps a true God is like true purple," she thought, "special, rich, and deep, worth looking for."

As Lydia grew up, her father started looking for a husband for her, but she shook her head.

"Give me some money instead," she said. "I know it's unusual for a woman, but I've worked hard for you and I know the cloth trade well. I'm going to move to Philippi, closer to the sea, and start my own business. I'm going to learn how to make true purple."

When Lydia arrived in Philippi, out of habit, she went to find the temples. There were more people wearing a true purple trim to their clothes here, and her eyes drank it in; only the most important people in society were allowed to wear such clothes. Some of them were priests at the temples, which were all dedicated to Greek gods and goddesses. Lydia looked at all the different names and statues, and she wondered again about the conversation she had overheard in Thyatira. What if there was one true God, better and more real than all of these, as true purple is to the madder root? Lydia summoned the courage to speak to one of the purple-trimmed men on the steps.

"Is there such a thing as a temple to one true God?" she asked. The man raised his eyebrows.

"The Jewish people worship what they call the one true God," he said, "but there aren't enough of them to have their own building. They meet by the river. I can show you the place."

From then on, Lydia set up her business, learning the trade of true purple, and building connections with the sellers of sea snails and the buyers of cloth. During that time, she attended meetings at least once a week by the river, with the people who believed in one true God. She wasn't the only Greek there; although people like her were not properly Jewish, they were welcome to listen to the Scriptures and to say that they believed, too.

Years went by, and Lydia's business grew. True purple was still rare, expensive, and sought-after, and selling it brought in plenty of money. One day, Lydia stood in the garden of her big house, watching her workers hang the dyed cloth out to dry. On every side she could see the glorious true purple, shining in the sun, billowing in the wind, rich and royal, and she knew that she had achieved her childhood dream.

Yet somehow, in a way she couldn't explain, something inside her was still searching. It was a feeling as if she'd been distracted while in the middle of some very important task, and now she couldn't remember what it was, only that she hadn't finished. She looked around her immaculate garden, the valuable cloth, the paintings on the walls of her elaborate mansion, full of empty rooms. What was it all for?

The next Sabbath day found Lydia by the riverside again, looking slightly more troubled than usual. She sat with the other women, many of whom were workers in her business, ready to listen. A man she had never seen before sat down with them and introduced himself as Paul. He said that he and his companions had seen a vision from God telling them to travel to Philippi, because somebody here needed to hear their message.

Lydia was fascinated. "Does the one true God really talk to people in visions and dreams?" she wondered.

"Definitely!" said Paul. "He speaks to us through the Holy Spirit, who is with us all the time, because of Jesus."

"Who is Jesus?" asked Lydia; and Paul told her how the one true God had sent his only Son to save all people and bring them close to him – not just Jews, but Greeks like Lydia too.

"Anybody who believes in Jesus and is baptized becomes a child of the one true God, and lives with Jesus for ever," declared Paul's friend Silas.

"We're sitting by the river," said Lydia. "Why not baptize us now?"

"Are you absolutely sure?" asked Paul. "We have plenty more to tell you!"

"I know true purple when I see it," said Lydia. "And I know the truth when I hear it. We'll get baptized now and talk later – at my house. You must stay with me. I insist."

So that's what happened. Lydia and all her workers were baptized, and the very first church in Philippi began in her house, as Paul and Silas told them all about Jesus, surrounded by swathes of true purple.

---

**Where does this story come from?**

*I have imagined the beginning of Lydia's life, but we do know that she was a seller of true purple cloth and that she came from Thyatira; and we know that*

*Thyatira was famous for the madder root purple. The rest of the story is found in Acts 16:11–15, and Lydia's house is mentioned again a bit later as the place that Paul and Silas went back to after they escaped (rather dramatically!) from prison.*

---

## What does it make you think about?

*Lydia was a very unusual woman. For a woman to own a business and a household without one reference to a husband was almost unheard of in ancient times. She must have been strong and determined. As a Greek woman worshipping with the Jewish community, she was a truth-seeker with an inquisitive, open mind. Telling her story reminded me of a parable that Jesus told about a merchant who saw a beautiful pearl and sold everything he had to own it. I think that Lydia, like that merchant, saw the value and beauty in God's kingdom and was determined to be a part of it. Does anything make you feel excited and passionate, like Lydia was about true purple? How does that compare with your feelings about God or something important in your life?*

Sample chapter from

## Louisa Freya, Dragon Slayer

# Clever Sigrun

There was once a girl called Sigrun who lived with her mother and father on the edge of an enormous farm. In those days, the farms were owned by squires, and people paid rent to grow crops on a little bit of the land. The squire who owned the land where Sigrun's family lived was extremely rich and not very pleasant, but as long as they worked as hard as they could and paid their share, they could keep their distance from the squire and be happy.

When she wasn't digging up potatoes or milking cows, Sigrun's favourite pastime was to ride her little grey pony, whose name was Jorunn. Jorunn was a quick and clever mare, who always seemed to know just what Sigrun was thinking.

One day, riding around their farm, Sigrun noticed that the crops didn't seem to be growing properly. When she got home and told her parents, they glanced worriedly at each other.

"There's been too much rain this year," said Sigrun's mother, "and the goat's stopped giving milk. I don't know how we're going to pay the rent without a good harvest."

"Well, I'll talk to the squire and see if he'll give us some more time to pay," said Sigrun. "He can't be as bad as all that, and anyway, we've never missed our rent before."

The next day, Sigrun rode Jorunn at a canter all the way up to the squire's huge house, and approached him as he took his morning walk around the garden.

"Please, sir," she said, "I've come to talk about my family's rent. Could we be given a little extra time to pay it? You see, the goat's stopped giving milk and…"

The squire, who had been looking Sigrun up and down while she was speaking, interrupted her.

"I'll write off the whole rent, my dear," he said, "if you will be my wife." And he smiled, except that only one side of his mouth got involved with the smile, and his eyes weren't smiling at all. Sigrun shuddered.

"Absolutely not – that will never happen, not ever at all!" she replied.

"What about your rent, then, little lady?"

"We'll manage somehow," said Sigrun, and she turned Jorunn's head toward home at a gallop.

Unfortunately, the idea of a wedding got itself into the head of the old squire, and before long he'd started talking to Sigrun's father, asking for Sigrun's hand in marriage in exchange for free rent and a new goat.

"What are we to do, Sigrun?" asked her father that evening. "I understand that you don't want to marry him, but it's a very tempting offer, and it would be a good marriage. He's very rich."

"I don't care if he can pile gold up to Jorunn's ears," declared Sigrun, "I'm not going to be his wife."

"He seems to admire you sincerely, too," said her father. "He asked so elegantly to be allowed to wed 'that beautiful visitor to my garden'."

Sigrun thought for a moment, then she smiled a wide smile.

"Father, tell him to send his servant boy down here next week to fetch the beautiful visitor to his garden. But he must use exactly those words, and nobody, not even the boy, must know the reason. If I'm going to be made to marry, I want to do it in secret."

"I'm so glad you've come around," said Sigrun's father, and the message was sent.

The squire was delighted and made lots of covert preparations. A week later, the boy appeared and found Sigrun polishing Jorunn's saddle.

"My master has sent me to collect the beautiful visitor to his garden, as you promised," he said with a bow.

"Oh, yes," Sigrun replied without looking up. "She's in the stable over there – I've got her all ready. I'll send over her saddle when I've finished cleaning it."

The boy frowned. "Are you sure? I thought..."
"Quite sure," smiled Sigrun. "She visited his garden less than a fortnight ago."

"All right then," said the boy, and he went to fetch Jorunn. He led the little grey pony up to the squire's mansion, where he found the squire very busy entertaining guests in the garden. Despite Sigrun's request for secrecy, he had invited all sorts of important people so that he could show off his new wife.

"I've got her, sir," called the boy.

"Great! Take her up to the best bedroom at once," answered the squire, without turning around.

The boy was puzzled. "And how am I supposed to do that?"

"Just get on with it, boy!" demanded the squire. "She can't be that much trouble!" He didn't so much as glance over his shoulder.

"Yes, sir!" sighed the boy.

With quite a lot of difficulty, the boy led Jorunn into the house, persuaded her up the stairs by placing a carrot at the top, and pushed her through the door of the best bedroom. There on the bed, a wedding dress was laid out, all lacy between garlands of flowers.

The boy leaned out of the window and shouted down into the garden. "She's in the bedroom, sir!"

"Excellent!" called the squire. "Now, make sure that she's dressed in all the clothes on the bed by noon!"

"And how am I supposed to do that?!" The squire was getting annoyed.

"Get the maids and the housekeeper to help you!"

The women were very surprised when they saw Jorunn in the best bedroom, but they knew better than to argue with a direct order from the squire, so they began to dress her up. The dress was a tight fit around the bride's neck, but the flower garlands looked lovely in her mane and tail, and the veil spread neatly across her back. The two little satin slippers had to go on her ears, since she had four big feet. At last, the housekeeper went to find the squire.

"She's all dressed, sir."

"Wonderful! Then bring her down the stairs into the garden!"

And so the beautiful visitor was brought clip-clopping into the garden once more, and when she saw the bridegroom standing among all his important visitors, she gave such a great snort that you'd have thought she was laughing. The squire jumped, stared, and looked from his bride to his guests and then back to his bride again. His face went radish red, then turnip purple. He took a deep breath, but just as he opened his mouth to say something, the bride reached forward and delicately helped herself to the flower in his lapel. With a shout of rage and disgust, he turned, ran into the house, and didn't come out until everyone had gone away. He was so embarrassed that he never mentioned either weddings or rent to Sigrun and her family again, so they and Jorunn all lived happily ever after.

## Where does this story come from?

*This funny story is a traditional Norwegian folk tale. It was collected by two writers called Asbjørnsen and Moe, who listened to lots of folk tales and wrote them down, just like the German brothers Grimm. They made many tales from Norway famous, and quite a few of them have female heroes – in fact, there is one other in this book. I had a bit of fun with the names for this story, since there weren't any in the original: Sigrun means "secret victory", and Jorunn is old Norse for "horse love"!*

## What does it make you think about?

*I wonder why we enjoy stories about proud, rich people being humiliated or not getting their way? I'm sure you can think of lots of others. It reminds me of some lines from the song that Mary, the mother of Jesus, sang before he was born, about what God was doing: "God brings down rulers from their thrones... God fills the hungry with good things, but he sends the rich away with nothing." (Luke 1:52–53). Perhaps when we laugh at the downfall of a proud, rich, and evil person in a story like this one – and feel good for Sigrun and her family – we're sharing a little bit in God's plan for the world.*